SELECTIONS FROM  O BROTHER, WHERE ART THOU?

Artwork and photos courtesy of Touchstone Pictures

Arranged by Jim Schustedt

ISBN 978-0-634-05978-0

HAL•LEONARD®
CORPORATION

7777 W. BLUEMOUND RD. P.O. BOX 13819 MILWAUKEE, WI 53213

Visit Hal Leonard Online at
www.halleonard.com

CONTENTS

The Big Rock Candy Mountain

Words, Music and Arrangement by Harry K. McClintock

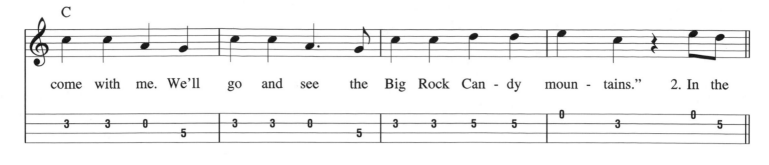

come with me. We'll go and see the Big Rock Can - dy moun - tains." 2. In the

Verse

Big Rock Can - dy moun - tains,__ there's a land that's fair and bright,__ where the
3., 4., 5. *See additional lyrics*

hand - outs grow on bush - es and you sleep out ev - 'ry night.___ Where the

box - cars all are emp - ty___ and the sun shines ev - 'ry day__ on the

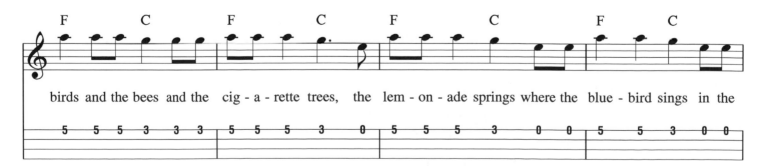

birds and the bees and the cig - a - rette trees, the lem - on - ade springs where the blue - bird sings in the

Outro

I'll see you all this com - in' fall _ in the Big Rock Can - dy moun - tains.

Additional Lyrics

3. In the Big Rock Candy mountains, all the cops have wooden legs
And the bulldogs all have rubber teeth and the hens lay soft boiled eggs.
The farmers' trees are full of fruit and the barns are full of hay.
Oh, I'm bound to go where there ain't no snow,
Where the rain don't fall, the wind don't blow
In the Big Rock Candy mountains.

4. In the Big Rock Candy mountains, you never change your socks
And the little streams of alcohol come a trickling down the rocks.
The brakeman have to tip their hats and the railroad bulls are blind.
There's a lake of stew and of whiskey too.
You can paddle all around 'em in a big canoe
In the Big Rock Candy mountains.

5. In the Big Rock Candy mountains, the jails are made of tin
And you can walk right out again as soon as you are in.
There ain't no short handled shovels, no axes, saws or picks.
I'm a goin' to stay where you sleep all day,
Where they hung the jerk that invented work,
In the Big Rock Candy mountains.

You Are My Sunshine

Words and Music by Jimmie Davis and Charles Mitchell

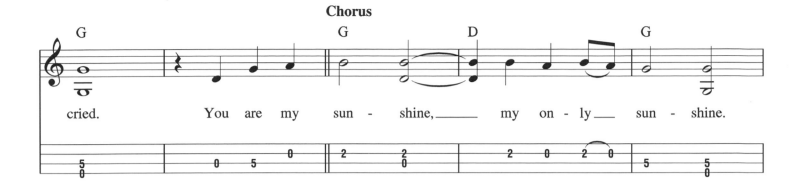

cried. You are my sun - shine, _____ my on - ly _____ sun - shine.

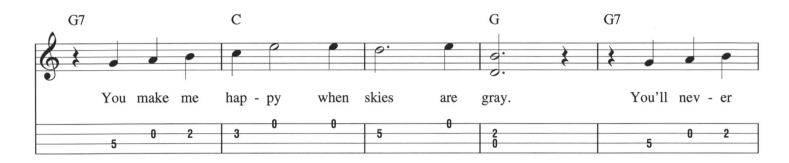

You make me hap - py when skies are gray. You'll nev - er

know dear _____ how much I love _____ you. Please don't take my

To Coda ⊕

* **Mandolin Solo (2nd time)**

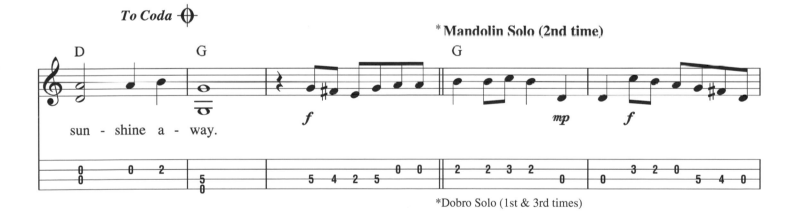

sun - shine a - way.

*Dobro Solo (1st & 3rd times)

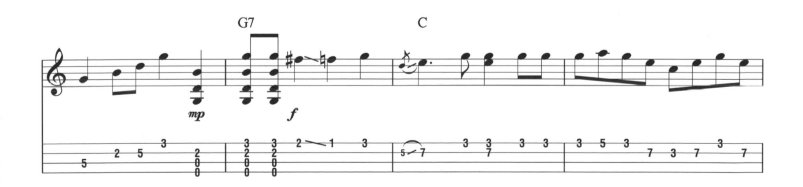

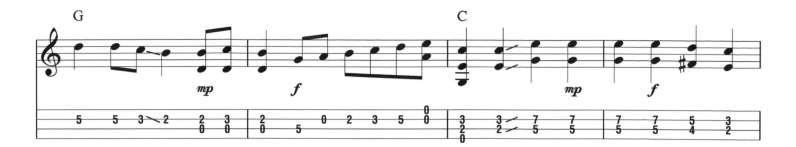

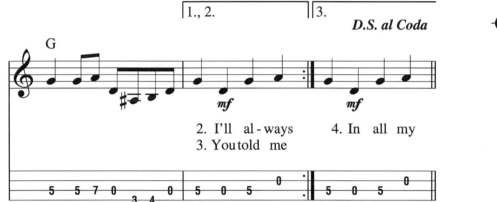

Outro

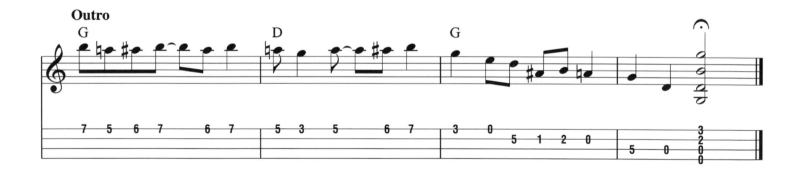

Additional Lyrics

2. I'll always love you and make you happy
   If you will only say the same.
   But if you leave me and love another,
   You'll regret it all some day.

3. You told me once, dear, you really loved me
   And no one could come between.
   But now you've left me to love another.
   You have shattered all of my dreams.

4. In all my dreams, dear, you seem to leave me.
   When I awake my poor heart pains.
   So won't you come back and make me happy.
   I'll forgive, dear, I'll take all the blame.

Down to the River to Pray

Traditional

Verse
Moderately

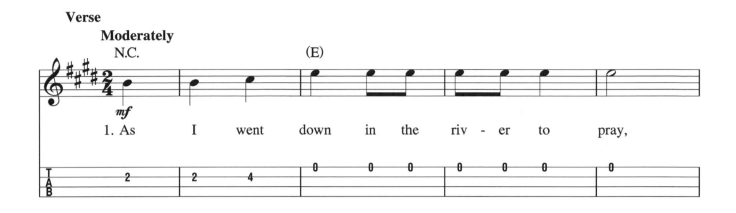

1. As I went down in the riv - er to pray,

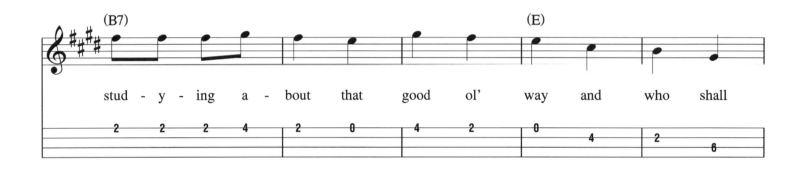

stud - y - ing a - bout that good ol' way and who shall

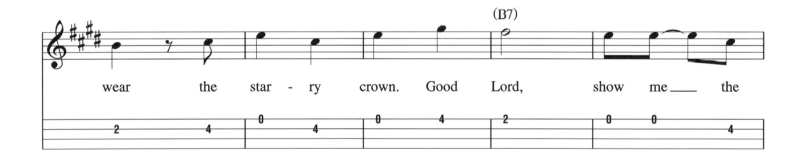

wear the star - ry crown. Good Lord, show me ___ the

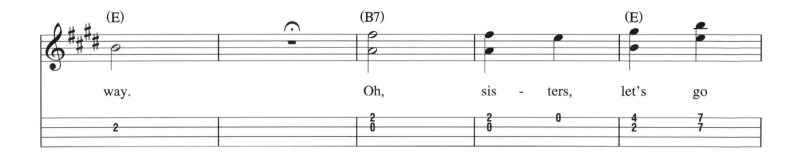

way. Oh, sis - ters, let's go

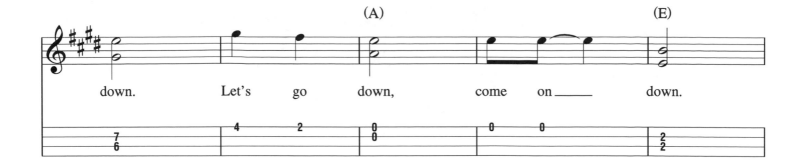

down. Let's go down, come on _____ down.

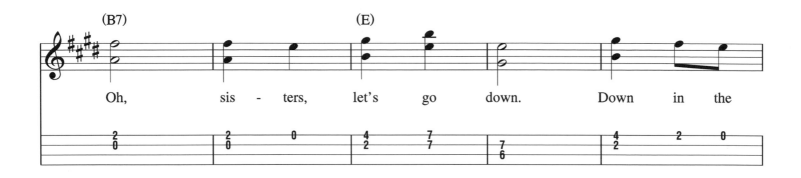

Oh, sis - ters, let's go down. Down in the

𝄋 Verse

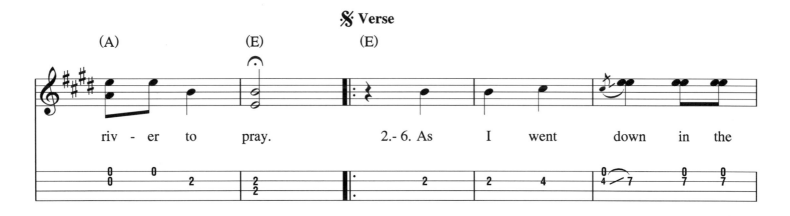

riv - er to pray. 2.- 6. As I went down in the

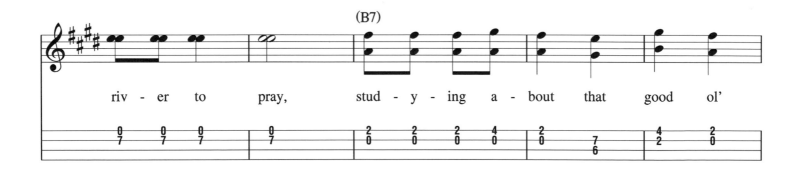

riv - er to pray, stud - y - ing a - bout that good ol'

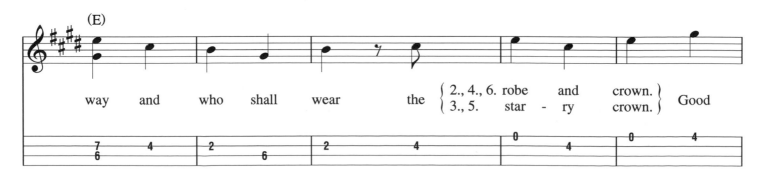

way and who shall wear the ⎰ 2., 4., 6. robe and crown. ⎱ Good
                                     ⎰ 3., 5. star - ry crown. ⎱

*5th time, *ritard*

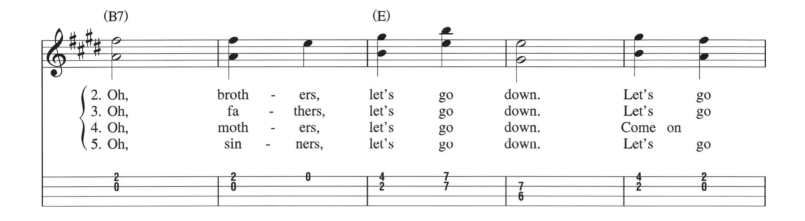

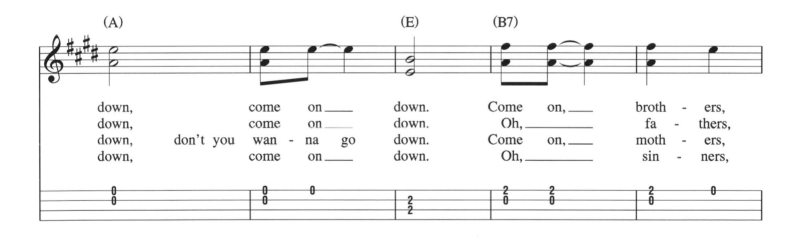

4th time, *D.S. al Fine*

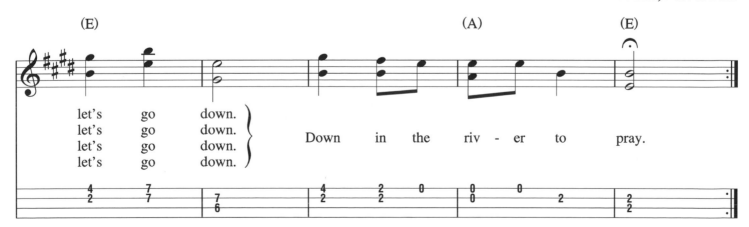

Keep on the Sunny Side

Words and Music by A.P. Carter

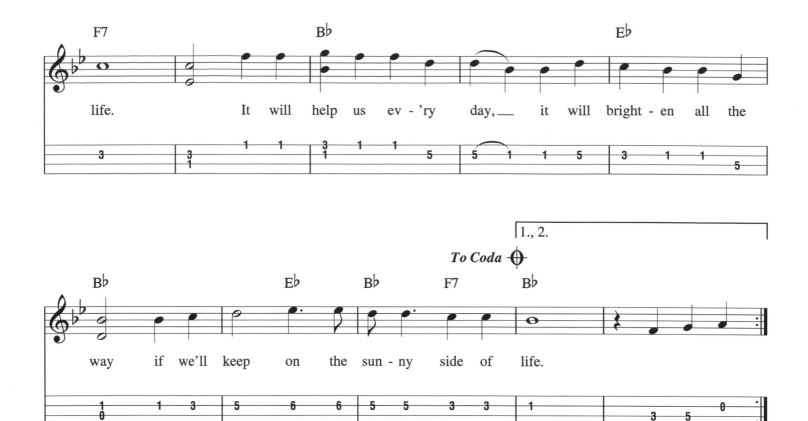

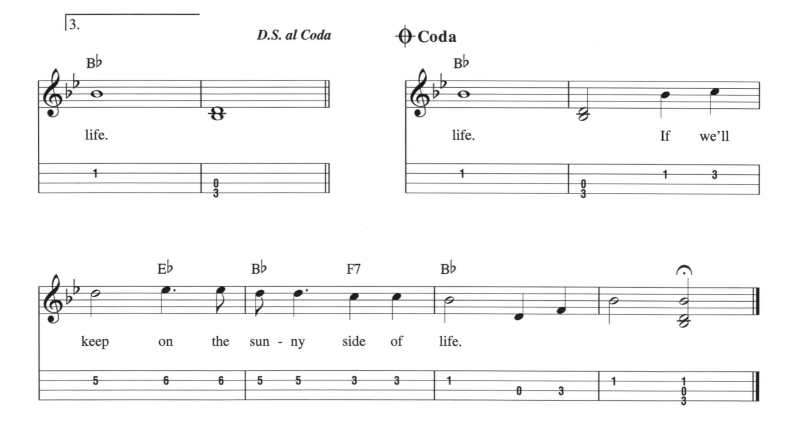

Additional Lyrics

2. Though the storm and its furies rage today
   Crushing hope that we cherish so dear,
   The cloud and storm will in time pass away
   And the sun again will shine bright and clear.

3. Let us greet with a song of hope each day
   Though the moment be cloudy or fair.
   And let us trust in our Savior always.
   He'll keep us, everyone, in His care.

I'll Fly Away

Words and Music by Albert E. Brumley

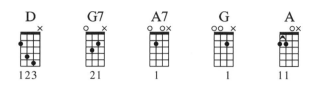

Mandolin Solo
Moderately

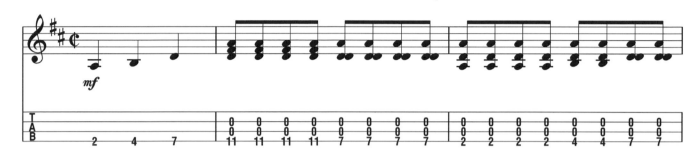

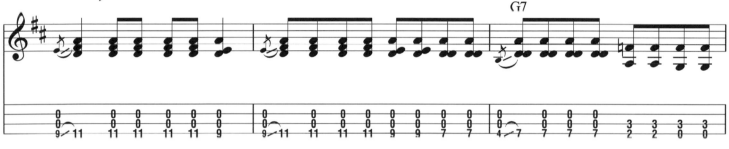

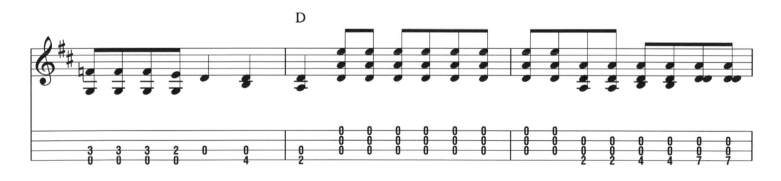

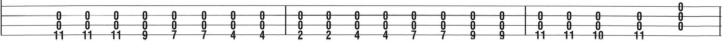

A7

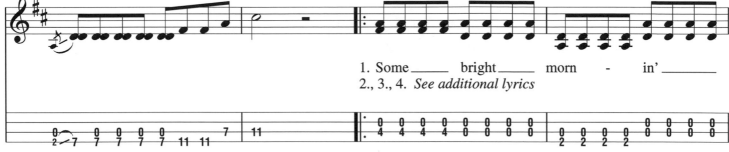

𝄋 **Verse**

D

D

1. Some_____ bright_____ morn - in'_____
2., 3., 4. *See additional lyrics*

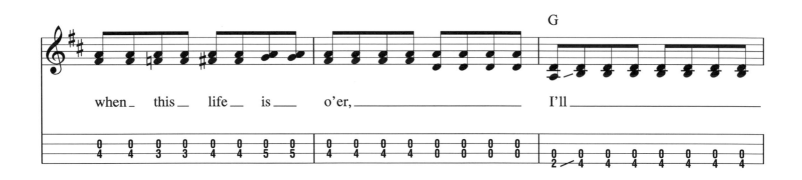

when_ this_ life_ is_____ o'er,_____ I'll_____

G

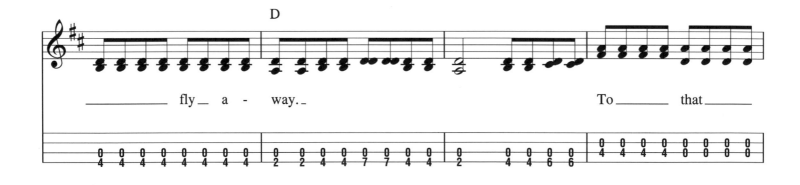

_____ fly_ a - way._____ To_____ that_____

D

home_____ on_____ God's_ ce - les - tial_ shore,

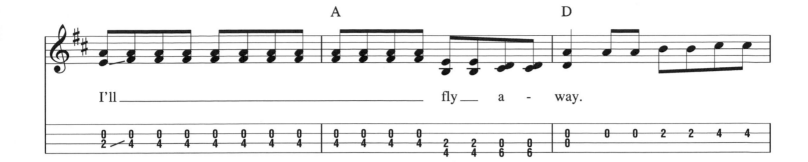

I'll _____ fly __ a - way.

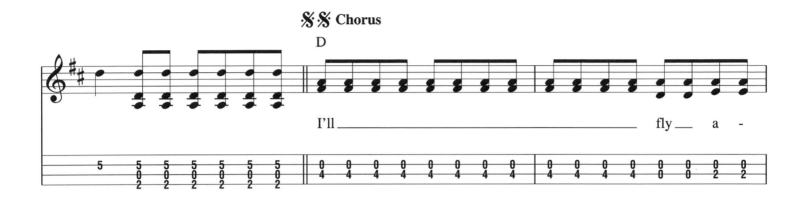

𝄋 𝄋 Chorus

I'll _____ fly __ a -

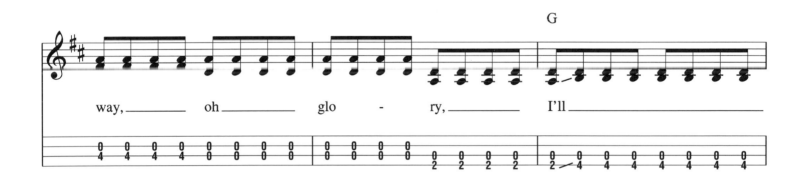

way, _____ oh _____ glo - ry, _____ I'll _____

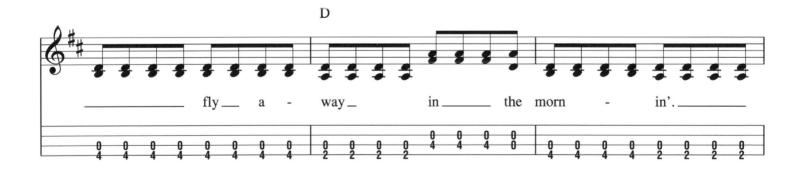

_____ fly __ a - way __ in _____ the morn - in'.

When _____ I _____ die, _____ hal - le - lu - jah by and __

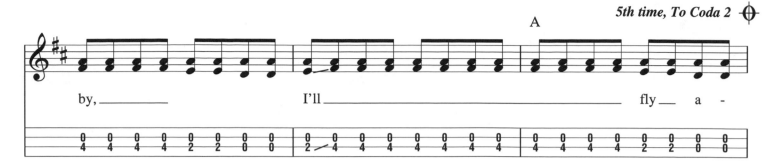

by, _____ I'll _____ fly __ a -

1. way. 2. way.

Mandolin Solo

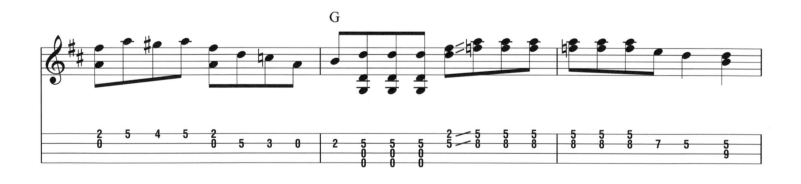

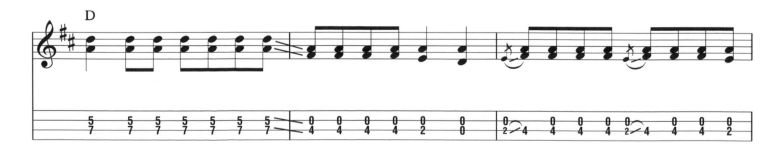

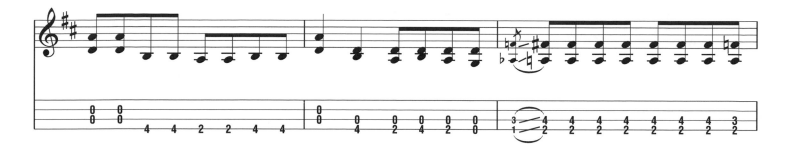

D.S. al Coda 1

⊕ Coda 1

Mandolin Solo

way.

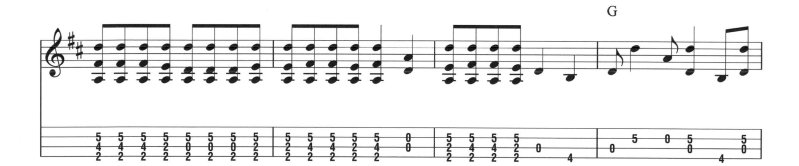

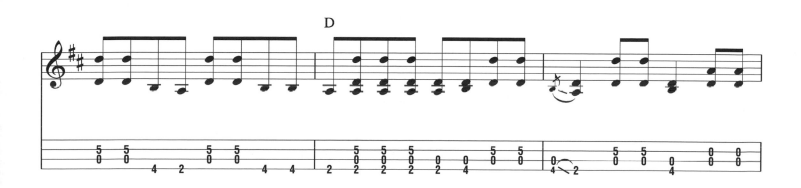

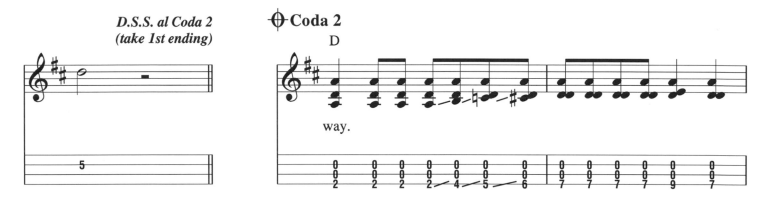

D.S.S. al Coda 2
(take 1st ending)

Coda 2

way.

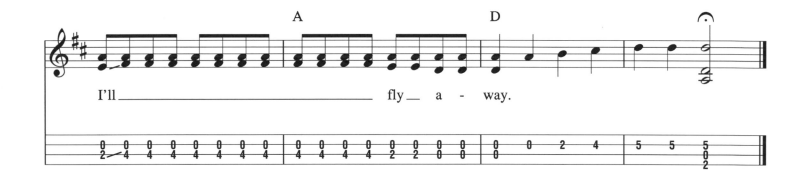

I'll _____ fly __ a - way.

Additional Lyrics

2. When the shadows of his life have gone,
   I'll fly away.
   Like a bird from these prison walls I'll fly.
   I'll fly away.

3. Oh, how glad and happy when we meet.
   I'll fly away.
   No more cold iron shackles on my feet.
   I'll fly away.

4. Just a few more weary days and then
   I'll fly away.
   To a land where joys will never end,
   I'll fly away.

In the Highways
(I'll Be Somewhere Working for My Lord)

Words and Music by Maybelle Carter

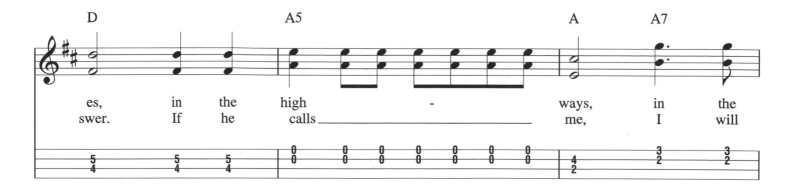

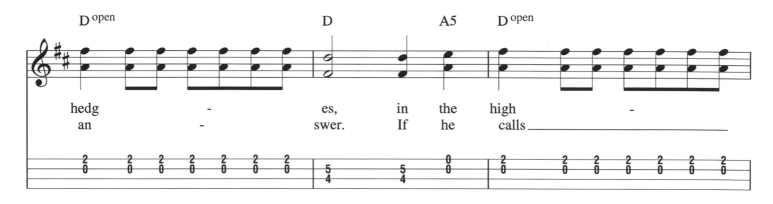

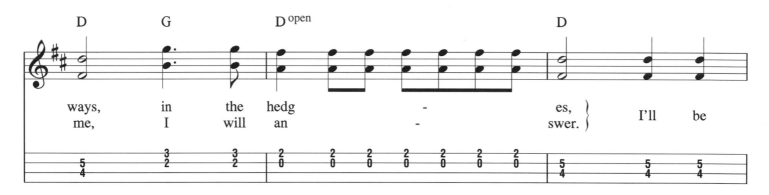

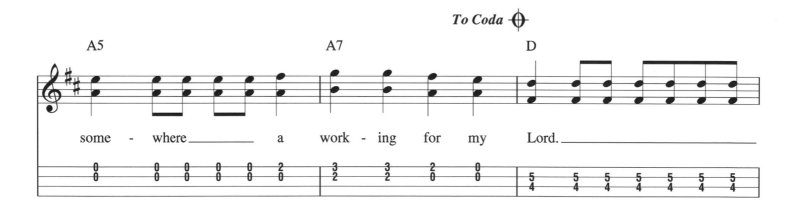

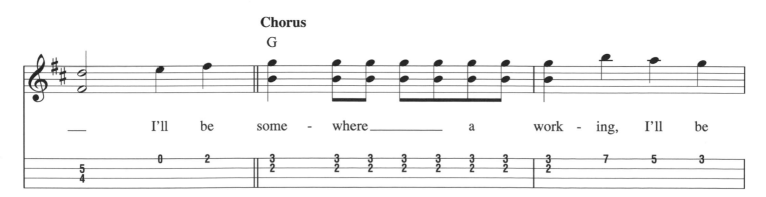

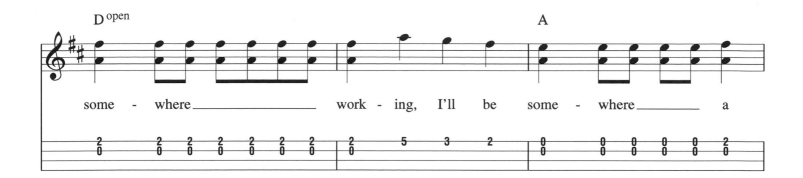

some - where _____ work - ing, I'll be some - where _____ a

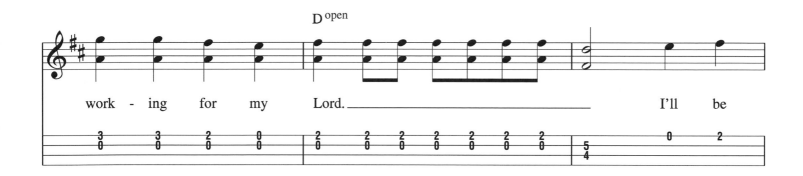

work - ing for my Lord. _____ I'll be

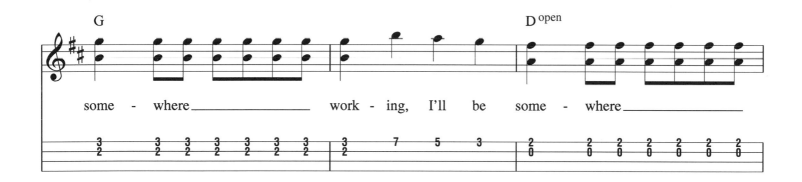

some - where _____ work - ing, I'll be some - where _____

work - ing, I'll be some - where _____ a work - ing for my

2nd time, D.S. al Coda
(take 1st lyrics)

 Coda

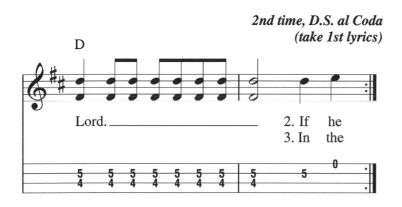

Lord. _____ 2. If he
3. In the

Lord.

I Am Weary (Let Me Rest)

Words and Music by Pete (Roberts) Kuykendall

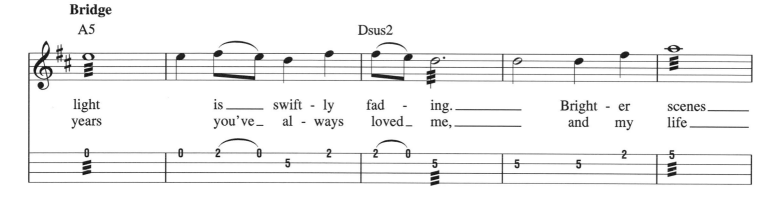

Bridge

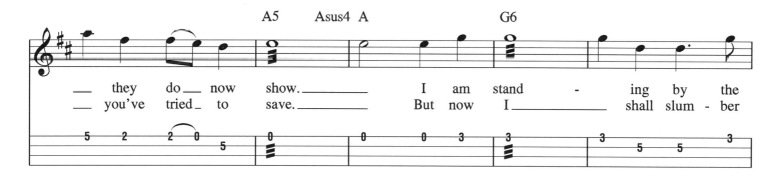

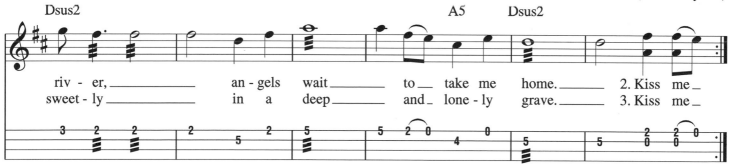

Coda

In the Jailhouse Now

Words and Music by Jimmie Rodgers

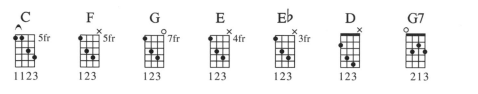

Tune down 1/2 step:
(low to high) Gb-Db-Ab-Eb

Intro
Moderately

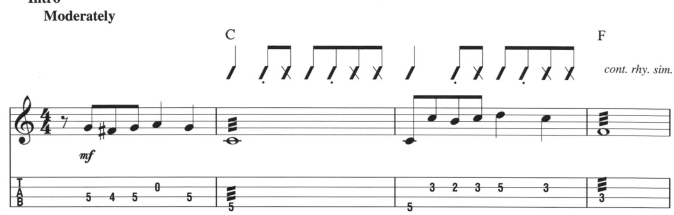

cont. rhy. sim.

Verse

1. I had a friend__ named Ram - bl - in' Bob.__ He used to steal,
2., 3. *See additional lyrics*

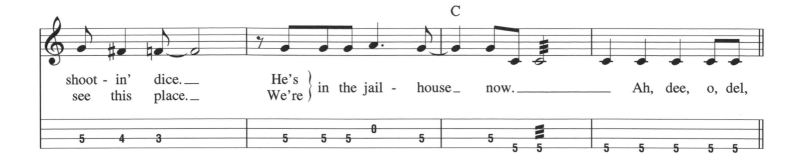

shoot - in' dice.__   He's } in the jail - house_ now._____ Ah, dee, o, del,
see this place._   We're }

Interlude

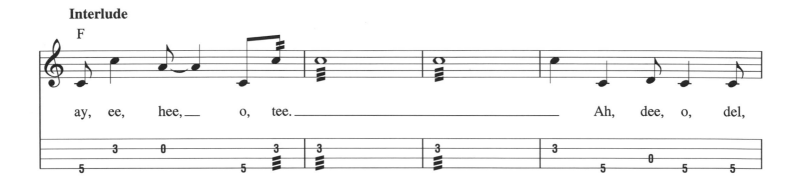

ay, ee, hee,__ o, tee._____ Ah, dee, o, del,

ay, ee, o,__ del, o, tee._____ Yo, del, ay, hee, hee,__ yo, del,

|1., 2. |3.

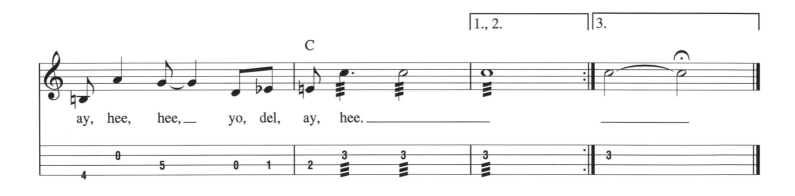

ay, hee, hee,__ yo, del, ay, hee._____   _____

Additional Lyrics

2. Bob liked to play his poker, pinochle, whist and euchre,
   But shootin' dice was his fav'rite game.
   Well, he got throwed in jail with nobody to go his bail.
   The judge done said that he refused the fine.

3. I went out last Tuesday. I met a girl named Susie.
   I said I was the swellest guy around.
   Well, we started to spendin' my money and she started to callin' me Honey.
   We took in ev'ry cabaret in town.

I Am a Man of Constant Sorrow

Words and Music by Carter Stanley

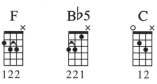

Mandolin Solo
Moderately

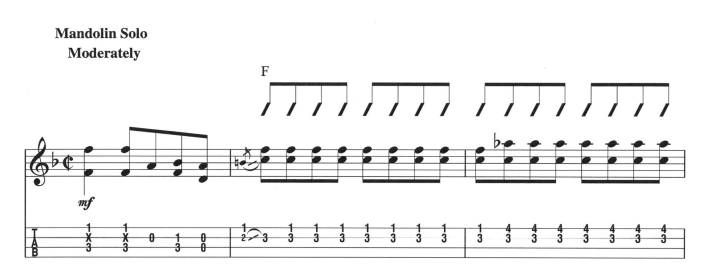

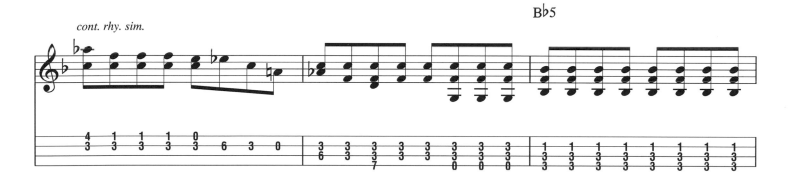

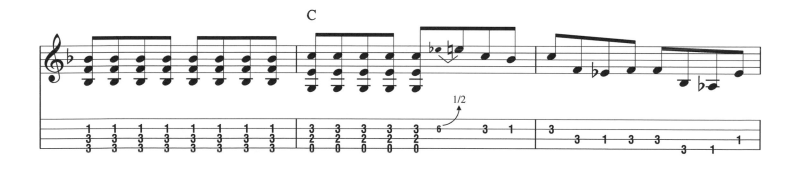

(In con- stant sor- row _____ all through_ his

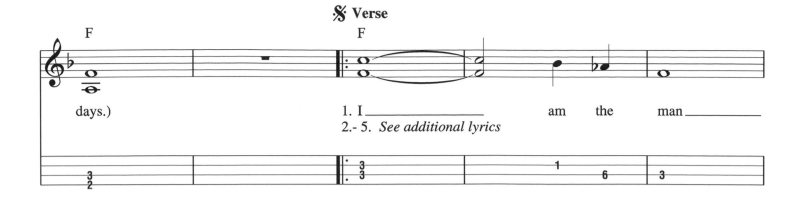

% **Verse**

days.)

1. I _____ am the man _____

2.- 5. *See additional lyrics*

— of con-stant sor-row. _____ I've seen trou - ble all of my

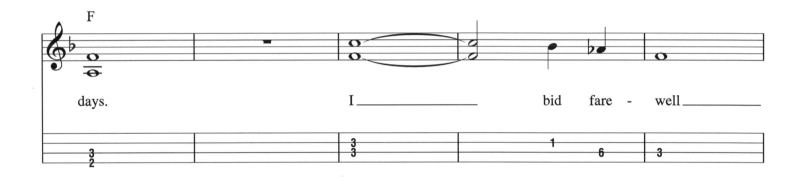

days. I _____ bid fare-well _____

— to old Ken-tuck-y, _____ the place where I _____ was born and

To Coda ⊕

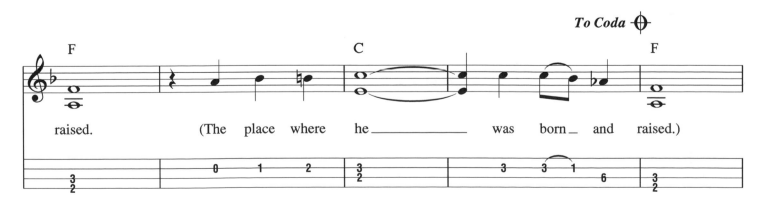

raised. (The place where he _____ was born_ and raised.)

* Mandolin Solo (3rd time)

*Dobro Solo (1st time),
Banjo Solo (2nd time),
Fiddle Solo (4th time)

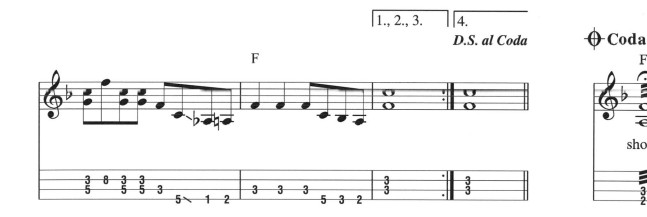

shore.)

Additional Lyrics

2. For six long years I've been in trouble,
No pleasure here on earth I've found.
For in this world I'm bound to ramble.
I have no friends to help me now.
(He has no friends to help him now.)

3. It's fare thee well, my own true lover.
I never expect to see you again.
For I'm bound to ride that northern railroad.
Perhaps I'll die upon that train.
(Perhaps he'll die upon this train.)

4. You can bury me in sunny valley
For many years where I may lay.
Pray and you may learn to love another
While I am sleeping in my grave.
(While he is sleeping in his grave.)

5. Maybe your friends think I'm just a stranger,
My face you never will see no more.
But there is one promise that is given,
I'll meet you on God's golden shore.
(He'll meet you on God's golden shore.)

Indian War Whoop

Words and Music by Hoyt Ming

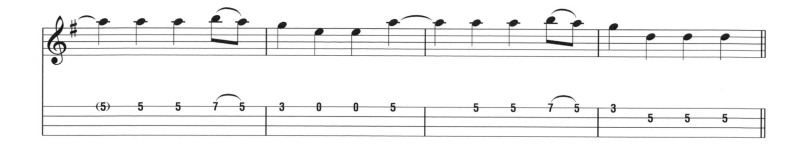

C

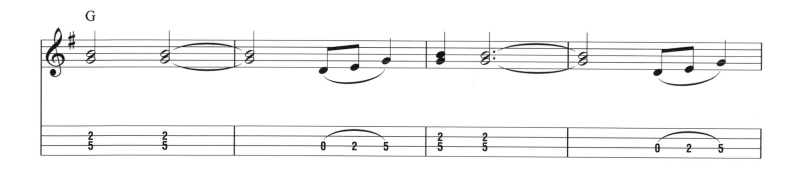

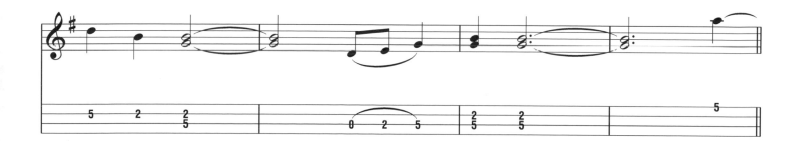

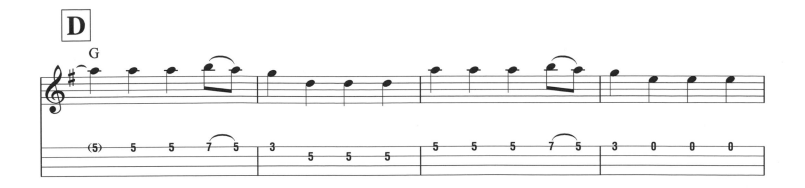

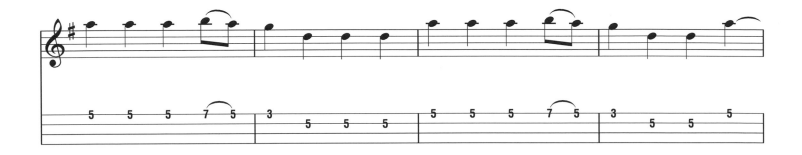

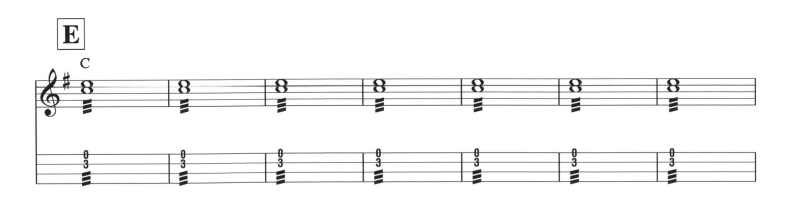

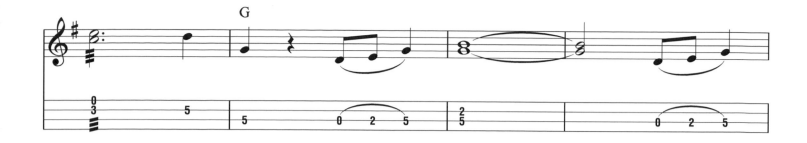

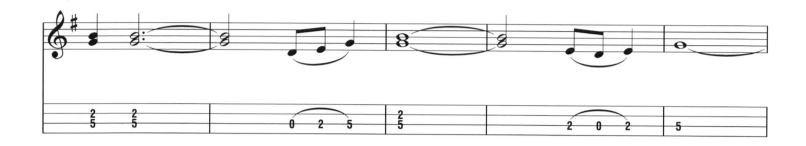

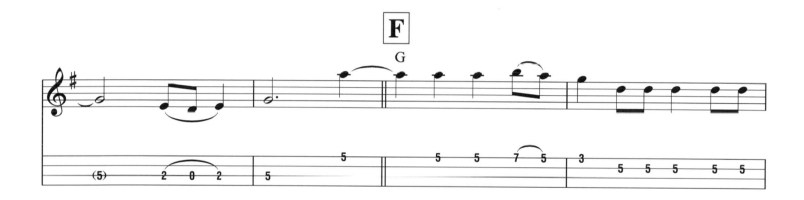

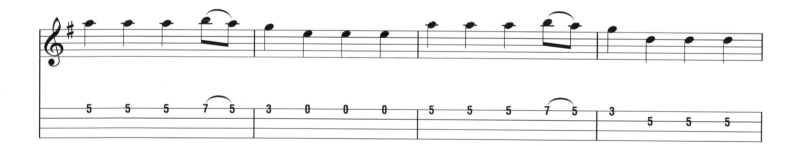

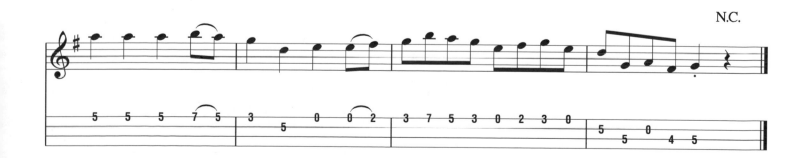

Angel Band

Words and Music by Ralph Stanley

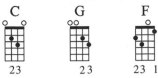

Tune down 1/2 step:
(low to high) G♭-D♭-A♭-E♭

Intro

Moderately

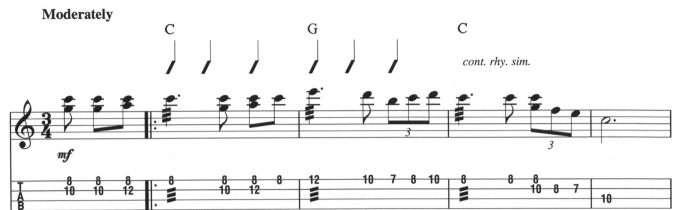

Verse

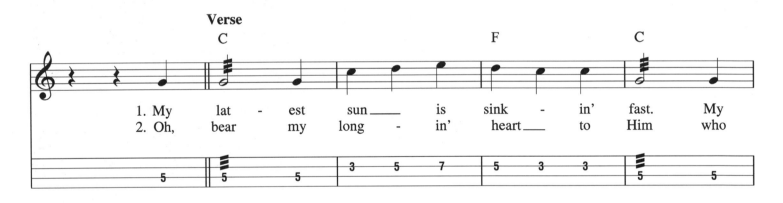

1. My lat - est sun ___ is sink - in' fast. My
2. Oh, bear my long - in' heart ___ to Him who

race is near - ly run. My strong - est tri - als
bled and died ___ for me, whose blood now cleans - es

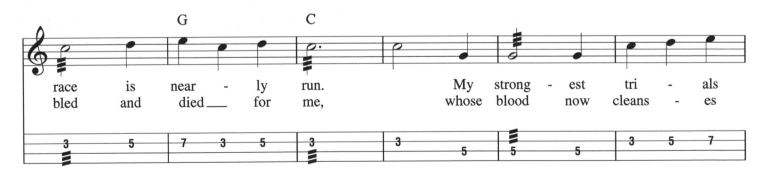

now ___ are past. My tri - umph has ___ be - gun.
from ___ all sin and gives me vic - to - ry.

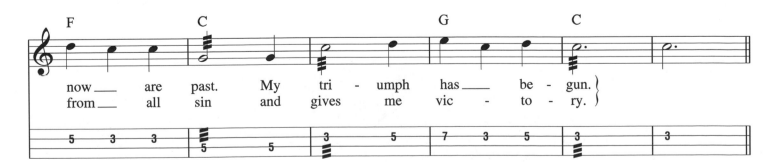

Chorus

Mandolin Notation Legend

Mandolin music can be notated three different ways: on a *musical staff*, in *tablature*, and in *rhythm slashes*.

RHYTHM SLASHES are written above the staff. Strum chords in the rhythm indicated. Use the chord diagrams found at the top of the first page of the transcription for the appropriate chord voicings.

THE MUSICAL STAFF shows pitches and rhythms and is divided by bar lines into measures. Pitches are named after the first seven letters of the alphabet.

TABLATURE graphically represents the mandolin fretboard. Each of the four horizontal lines represents each of the four courses of strings, and each number represents a fret.

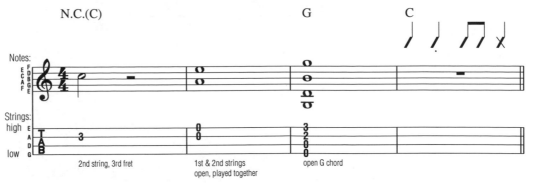

2nd string, 3rd fret | 1st & 2nd strings open, played together | open G chord

Definitions for Special Mandolin Notation

MUTED STRING(S): Lightly touch a string with the edge of your fret-hand finger while fretting a note on an adjacent string, causing the muted string to be unheard. Muting all of the strings with the fingers of the fret-hand while strumming the strings with the picking hand produces a percussive effect.

HAMMER-ON: Strike the first (lower) note with one finger, then sound the higher note (on the same string) with another finger by fretting it without picking.

PULL-OFF: Place both fingers on the notes to be sounded. Strike the first note and, without picking, pull the finger off to sound the second (lower) note.

LEGATO SLIDE: Strike the first note and then slide the same fret-hand finger up or down to the second note. The second note is not struck.

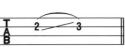

SHIFT SLIDE: Same as the legato slide except the second note is struck.

HALF-STEP BEND: Strike the note and bend up ½ step.

GRACE NOTE BEND: Strike the note and immediately bend up as indicated.

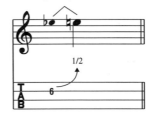

TREMOLO PICKING: The note is picked rapidly and continuously.

Additional Musical Definitions

p *(piano)*	• Play quietly.
mp *(mezzo-piano)*	• Play moderately quiet.
mf *(mezzo-forte)*	• Play moderately loud.
f *(forte)*	• Play loudly.
cont. rhy. sim.	• Continue strumming in similar rhythm.
N.C. *(no chord)*	• Don't strum until the next chord symbol. Chord symbols in parentheses reflect implied harmony.
D.S. al Coda	• Go back to the sign (𝄋), then play until the measure marked ***"To Coda"***, then skip to the section labeled ***"Coda."***
D.S.S. al Coda 2	• Go back to the double sign (𝄋𝄋), then play until the measure marked ***"To Coda 2"***, then skip to the section labeled ***"Coda 2."***
D.S. al Fine	• Go back to the sign (𝄋), then play until the label ***"Fine."***

	*(staccato)*	• Play the note or chord short.
rit.	*(ritard)*	• Gradually slow down.
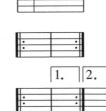	*(fermata)*	• Hold the note or chord for an undetermined amount of time.
		• Repeat measures between signs.
		• When a repeated section has different endings, play the first ending only the first time and the second ending only the second time.

NOTE: Tablature numbers in parentheses mean:
1. The note is being sustained over a system (note in standard notation is tied), or
2. The note is sustained, but a new articulation (such as a hammer-on, pull-off or slide) begins.